Where Seagulls Go To Be Lonely

by
Mark Nicholls

This first edition published in Australia in 2019 by:

Prahran Publishing
P.O. Box 2041, Prahran, Victoria, 3181

© Copyright Mark Nicholls 2019

Mark Nicholls has asserted his legal and moral right under the Copyright Act 1968 to be identified as the author of this work.

Published by arrangement with
Prahran Publishing, Australia.

All rights are strictly reserved.

No part of this publication may be reproduced, stored in a retrieval system or transmitted, in any form or by any other means, without the publisher's prior permission in writing. Copying of this script for performance reasons is also strictly prohibited by law, either in whole or excerpts from.

This book is sold subject to the condition that it shall not, by way of trade or otherwise, be lent, resold, hired out or otherwise circulated without the publisher's prior consent in any form of binding or cover other than that in which it is published and without similar condition, including this condition, being imposed on the subsequent purchaser.

Every reasonable effort has been made to trace copyright holders of material reproduced in this book, but if any have been inadvertently overlooked the publishers would be glad to hear from them. The story, all names, characters, and incidents portrayed in this book are fictitious. No identification with actual persons past or present, places, buildings, and products is intended or should be inferred.

ISBN 978-1-922263-10-0 Paperback
ISBN 978-1-922263-11-7 eBook

Dewey: 822.4

 A catalogue record for this book is available from the National Library of Australia

Performance Licensing and Royalty Payments

Mark Nicholls retains control of both the amateur and professional stage performance rights of this play. No unauthorised performance should occur without the express and written permission of the playwright.

Restriction of Alteration

There shall be no modifications of any kind to the play including deletion of dialogue (including objectionable language), changes to characters gender or names, title of the play or music without the express and written permission from the author.

Sound and Video Recordings

This play may contain stage directions to include the use of music, video or other sound recordings either in part or in whole. The author and the publisher have not sought the right to use such content and performance rights permission should be obtained seperately. Permission to record audio and video recordings of all performances must also be explicitly given by the author in writing.

Author Credit

Performance rights approval requires credit be given to Mark Nicholls as the sole and exclusive author of the play. This obligation applies to the title page of every program or other advertising material distributed in connection to this play. The author's credit should appear immediately under the title of the play on all published material, and alongside no other individual. Font size of credit cannot be less than 50% of the largest letter used in the play's title.

Please email info@prahran.press
for all performance enquiries.

Dedication

for Oscar Wirtz

About the Playwright

MARK NICHOLLS has been performing on various Melbourne stages since the age of six and has an extensive list of credits as a playwright, composer, singer, actor, producer and director. He is Senior Lecturer in Cinema Studies at the University of Melbourne where he has taught film since 1993.

He is the author of *Lost Objects of Desire: The Performances of Jeremy Irons* (2012), *Scorsese's Men: Melancholia and the Mob* (2004) and recently published articles on Italian Cinema, Powell and Pressburger's *The Red Shoes* and Sergei Diaghilev's celebrated company, The Ballets Russes.

Mark is a film critic and worked for many years on ABC Radio and for *The Age* newspaper, for which he wrote a weekly column between 2007 and 2009.

He lives in Melbourne with his partner, Ali Wirtz, and their two sons Oscar and Carlo.

Series Preface

I wrote these plays for only one reason, to perform them. I publish them here, therefore, somewhat reluctantly. They were never written to be read on the page by anyone but a treasured posy of performers that I trust to help me rescue them from it. They were certainly never conceived of as works of anything so respectable as literature. Nevertheless, I have found two reasons to overcome my reluctance and my usual roguish prejudice against readers and writers in favour of performers and punters. One reason is that putting these plays into print provides the opportunity for the most engaged of those who saw and heard them to revive and revise the experience. The other reason is archival. I wish to leave a permanent, if inadequate, record of the facts of their production over a decade, in a private space in Melbourne, for the benefit of both a small, dedicated paying audience, and for a smaller band of compulsive show-folk.

Writing these plays for the talented actors, musicians and backstage characters whose creations are recorded here, and having the privilege of working with these artists to produce them, has been the most satisfying occupation of my otherwise horrendously charmed and fascinating life.

Now that they have had their blessed release in print, these plays are beyond the concern of any motivation I had to write them. Read them, o curious one, and work it out for yourself! One motivation I will record, however, rests in the inspiration generously given by those who worked on and attended these cosy performances, and so brought their privileged, fleeting moments of theatre securely into being.

About the Play

The longer I think about a play or film, the more difficulty I have in believing that it is about anything much other than the process of its own making. To unprejudiced eyes, *Hiroshima Mon Amour* may look like a film about the crisis of mutually assured destruction. *Life is Beautiful* may easily be read as a film about the atrocity of the Holocaust. To me, after so many years of watching, studying and teaching these 'texts', as Martin Scorsese says of his own bloodbath scene in *Taxi Driver*, 'all I see is the technique'. In the apparent pursuit of solutions to superhuman problems like nuclear destruction or genocide, I find it almost impossible to see past the cast and crew going about their business, carrying on in the all too human ways that they have to simply to get the job done. To me *The Rite of Spring* can never be a tale of ancient Scythian rituals and the human sacrifice of a virgin dancing herself to death. For a leading dancer, this ballet is simply an account of what she has to put up with every day at work.

The major exception to this is the backstage comedy-drama. This is the one place where I think shows take life seriously. If you really want to know what is going on at the law firm, hospital or university where you work, spend an afternoon with

Singin' in the Rain or John Osborne's *The Entertainer*. Next time you fall in love, you may as well forget Netflixing *Love Story* or taking a punt on *Romeo and Juliet* in the Botanic Gardens. *Stan and Ollie* or the Gilbert and Sullivan romance, *Topsy-Turvy*, will tell you all you need to know about loving another person, and why we keep coming back for more.

Sometimes Federico Fellini used to put out a notice telling the world that he was about to make a film and would be happy to hear from anyone who was interested in joining him. The resulting film would be very much about those who showed up. Thinking of other directors like Orson Welles and Peter Sellars, I suspect this type of approach is more common to show-making than many showfolk are prepared to admit. This isn't quite my method, nor can I hope to be compared to Fellini, Welles or Sellars in any way, but it seems to me that making performance works in this way is just as good a method as any other. The theatre of ideas and a commitment to values of social justice or environmental awareness doesn't have to begin with the intellectual-as-playwright hiding away on a laptop. Nor does it need to end with the intellectual-as-critic lost down the same antisocial rabbit hole.

With a view to reviving our previous five productions, we invited two highly talented actors, Evangeline Stoios and Helena Duniec, to join us at Rear Four in late 2015. Happily, this did nothing for our revivalist plans, but it had the pleasing effect of bringing on two new plays, this one and *The Gentle Rain from Heaven*, which followed it in 2017. *Where Seagulls go to be Lonely* was thus certainly the result of Helena and Evangeline showing up. It was also the result of us dragging in Gwendolen Swain to play her bit so marvellously in the last act. As a play about showfolk and created in such conditions, I think it probably says more about real life and work and love and getting up in the morning, than almost anything we have done, or are likely to do.

CHARACTERS

HELENA: a fifty-five-year-old (or so she says)

EMMELINE: a twenty-three-year-old, her daughter

VIOLET: a twenty-one-year-old, her friend

WEBB: a fifty-year-old

MADELEINE: a fast-talking twelve-year-old.

SETTING

Here and recently with a gap of some months and another of some years.

Where Seagulls Go To Be Lonely *was first performed at Rear 4, Clifton Hill, Victoria on the 2nd of March 2016 with the following cast:*

Helena: Madeleine Swain

Emmeline: Evangeline Stoios

Violet: Helena Duniec

Webb: Mark Nicholls

Madeleine: Gwendolen Swain

Director:	Mark Nicholls
Stage Manager:	Oscar Wirtz
Assistant Stage Manager:	Carlo Nicholls
Co Producer:	Alison Wirtz

ACT ONE

It's about 7.30pm. EMMELINE is rushing about madly, preparing a stage area and props for a performance of some sort. VIOLET, a pattern of indolence, is sitting on a chair downstage left. She occasionally casts a glance towards what EMMELINE is doing. Completely preoccupied, she neither feels nor demonstrates any inclination to help.

VIOLET: I'm not doing anything at all!

EMMELINE: Yes you are. Of course, you are.

VIOLET: What do you mean?

EMMELINE: You are preparing. I want you completely focused, with all your energy in store for the performance. Then when she gets here you can unleash yourself at her.

VIOLET: Are you sure your mother really wants to be unleashed at?

EMMELINE: She's bound to, once she sees you in action. But it is important that you do it exactly the way you did it when we rehearsed it on Monday.

VIOLET: But I was absolutely exhausted by that rehearsal.

EMMELINE: I know, you were marvellous. *[She rushes up to her, grabs her by the cheeks and kisses her like her life depended on it]* It was thrilling. I was so excited by the way you did it. I just fell in love with you all over again.

VIOLET: Really? I wish you wouldn't.

EMMELINE: But I can't help myself if I am in love with you.

VIOLET: Don't make jokes about it. It really makes me uncomfortable when you kiss me like that and go all gay for me.

EMMELINE: But I am absolutely mad about you when you do my play. I love you, I love you, I love you. And I love art and theatre and the rush the whole thing gives me. I don't care about all that disgusting pairing off business. You know, boyfriends and girlfriends and sex nonsense. When you play this part, I am filled with excitement and the only thing I can possibly think of to call it is love, L-O-V-E, love.

VIOLET: So, what was all the business in your bedroom with James I heard about two the other morning?

EMMELINE: Well, we are working on our new journal.

VIOLET: It wasn't exactly the dulcet tones of joint publication that I was hearing through the wall.

EMMELINE: Oh that. The inevitable expenditure of pent-up intellectual energy. There's nothing in it at all.

VIOLET: So that's not love?

EMMELINE: Strictly academic and literary, therefore, nothing to do with romance.

VIOLET: You could use that as your mission statement.

EMMELINE: What do you mean?

VIOLET" 'Strictly academic and literary, therefore, nothing to do with romance.' It's a perfectly adequate summary of your new theatre journal.

EMMELINE: Ah, the caustic remark with amusing intent. But it is not caustic or amusing, its one hundred percent accurate. Strictly academic and literary, therefore, nothing to do with romance.

VIOLET: Really? That's where you want to go?

EMMELINE: That's exactly where we want to go. We are not interested in the theatre of romance and all that sentimental nonsense my mother has been trotting out all these years. We are interested in the theatre of ideas, and dangerous ideas at that. An evening in the theatre should be... No. Why should it be 'an evening in the theatre'? Sounds like a bunch of old farts frocking up for 'an evening at the opera'. That's not theatre. It's the expensive acquisition of high culture talking points ready for easy incision into polite conversations about Botox and *[thinking of it]* holidays in Broome. Theatre should happen anywhere and at any time. Just as we are doing it, right here and right now. It shouldn't be... It can't be confined to judiciously subsidised spaces and arts festivals. And it mustn't be about entertainment and stars and all that contrived stagy business and gags. Experiencing great theatre should be the next best thing to sitting down quietly and calmly to read a really good book. And not one of those girly page turners that everybody's so keen on, with large print. Theatre should be like a really strong and thought-provoking, academic discourse.

VIOLET: Yes, I can see that.

EMMELINE: *[Missing Violet's sarcasm]* I knew you understood. That's why you are so good in this play. You get it.

VIOLET: Yes. Obviously I'm brilliant. But do you think other people will see it that way? You know, ordinary people that just want a fun evening out.

EMMELINE: Well, if that's their attitude they are obviously not going to get it. I can't be interested in them anyway.

VIOLET: How does your mother see it?

EMMELINE: Who cares about her?

VIOLET: Well, obviously the theatre-going public do. Or did.

EMMELINE: Oh yes I know, Dame Helena! Filling the commercial theatres every night with polite inner-city subscribers and every Wednesday matinee with Bendigo busloads. Don't worry about her. When the revolution comes, she'll be the first to go.

VIOLET: That's a bit harsh, isn't it? I can see she's settled into a fairly comfortable regime of 'comedy classics' but she's always been pretty much at the cutting edge of things?

EMMELINE: I thought you had never met her?

VIOLET: I haven't, but I have read about her.

EMMELINE: I don't think *TV WEEK* really requires all that much reading, do you?

VIOLET: I'm not talking about all that.

EMMELINE: Well, what are you talking about?

VIOLET: I had to do an essay on Australian theatre in first semester...

EMMELINE: Oh God. Performance Studies!

VIOLET: Yes Performance Studies – and she comes up quite a bit in the early days – you know the 1990s! She was obviously heavily involved in some really interesting stuff.

EMMELINE: What Noel Coward revivals and 'edgy' modern dress Shakespeare?

VIOLET: No. She was into some really key things. I read somewhere that she was one of the founders of the Rear Four Movement.

EMMELINE: Yeah right. Amateur theatricals in a comfy salon setting, don't remind me.

VIOLET: It sounds quite interesting to me.

EMMELINE: I had to sell the tickets and move the furniture. Believe me, it wasn't anything like 'interesting'. And when did it become 'the Rear Four Movement' anyway? 'Rear Four' was just a pretentious way of saying 'up the lane and out the back at Mum's place'. It wasn't cutting edge; it was convenience. The council had to close it down eventually because too many people complained that we were running a North Fitzroy brothel. Which is exactly what it was.

VIOLET: Well, my lecturer seemed quite interested in it. I got an 'A'.

EMMELINE: That is absolutely infuriating.

VIOLET: What do you mean? I get 'A's all the time.

EMMELINE: Not that. Of course you got an 'A'. To get an 'A' in the Art Faculty at Melbourne Uni all you really need to do is come from a private school and not start any sentence with 'because'.

VIOLET: Thanks very much.

EMMELINE: It's infuriating because that is so typical of Helena. And it is 'Helëna', by the way, not Helena. She only started with that Helena business when she got into the newspapers. Where she came from, if she had tried getting away with any affectation like that, the locals would have lynched her, God bless 'em. No, it's infuriating, because my mother is basically just a hack like thousands of other would-bes who never get anywhere. She has no talent, no subtlety and no theatrical brain at all. She just has this annoying ability to tap into whatever

> *The Age* lifestyle section wants to determine to be the zeitgeist. The result being that everyone from the pie seller at the MCG to the Dean of Arts at ANU thinks she's fantastic.

VIOLET: You'd have to say that is a talent.

EMMELINE: See what I mean? Even you are mad about her.

VIOLET: I am not mad about her. I've never even met her. I just think her career sounds interesting.

EMMELINE: Well, it's not. And I am really disappointed in you if you think it is. You are ten times the actor she ever was and it is really absurd if you can't see that.

VIOLET: Do you really think so? I don't know. I feel so wooden on stage and all I really think I am doing is trying to remember the lines and not get all the other stuff wrong.

EMMELINE: Don't worry about the other stuff for now. It's my lines that count. I want you to do it exactly that way. I don't want anyone to think you are some person in the real world. I want you to be an *[gesturing]* 'actor' on stage, speaking the lines that the *[gesturing]* 'writer' has given you. I don't want my lines to reek of anything real.

VIOLET: I wouldn't worry about that.

> *We hear the front door opening and the beginnings of distant chatter.*

EMMELINE: Good. Anyway, that is them back from the pub. Quick, I want you frozen in place on your mark. I don't want them to have any time to realise what is happening. They must be totally unprepared.

VIOLET: OK.

VIOLET moves to the centre of the stage area. She stands next to a stool and raises one foot on it before freezing. She is obviously not comfortable with the entire business. EMMELINE takes her place waiting for them to enter from the hall. She is full of manic excitement and takes a large breath.

WEBB: *[Off and obviously full in every sense]* I always feel full after that chicken parma. I told you not to let me have the chips.

HELENA: *[Off and also obviously full in every sense]* You have only yourself to blame. You have absolutely no restraint.

WEBB: *[Off]* That coming from you!

WEBB and HELENA enter.

EMMELINE: Webb, Helena, I have something for you. Don't say anything. Just stand and watch what is about to happen.

HELENA: Darling, you should have come with us to the...

EMMELINE: Mother, please.

HELENA: What's the matter? What's happened? You look terrible.

WEBB: You do Emmy. Can I get you anything?

EMMELINE: Please both of you. Don't say anything. Just look over there and listen.

HELENA: What are you... Oh hello. I didn't realise anyone else was here. You must be a friend of Emmy's? I'm Helena and this is...

HELENA breaks out of her frozen pose for a second as it would be rude not to say hello.

EMMELINE: Mother, please. Violet! It doesn't matter who this is. This is a performance. Just be quiet and let it happen.

HELENA: Oh. Right. Sorry. But I can't possibly sit just now. I really need a glass of water and the loo. Can you just wait a second and I'm all yours.

HELENA makes for the kitchen and a glass of water.

EMMELINE: No Mum, it can't wait. The theatre of ideas can't stop for anything.

HELENA: Well, I am afraid it is going to have to stop for a moment dear. I'm mad about the theatre of ideas and I firmly believe you can always fight city hall, but I don't intend to fight the call of nature.

HELENA exits left.

EMMELINE: Oh, for fuck's sake.

EMMELINE exits right. VIOLET remains in her position and WEBB stands waiting for something to happen. Nothing does for quite some time. Finally, VIOLET begins the play.

VIOLET: "Stretches of tall, roughly-cut barbed wire intermittently skewer the afternoon sky. *[A pause]* A lone cloud is pierced but produces no rain."

We hear a toilet flush. VIOLET looks increasingly uncomfortable.

VIOLET: "A sick dog on the perimeter barks at an illusion."

WEBB: Sorry to interrupt, but are you enjoying yourself?

VIOLET: Not really.

WEBB: I'm sure it would be all right if you stopped. I'm quite enjoying it, but you don't look as if you are and there's no one here.

VIOLET: No. I will stop. If you don't mind?

WEBB: It's fine.

There is more silence as VIOLET comes

slowly out of character.

WEBB: I'm Cliff.

VIOLET: I thought I heard someone just called you 'Webb'.

WEBB: They did. Or rather they do. Anyway, call me Webb if you like.

VIOLET: I'm Violet. I house share with Emmeline.

WEBB moves to shake her hand.

WEBB: It's nice to meet you.

VIOLET: You too.

They shake hands.

WEBB: We've just been having lunch at the pub.

VIOLET: Yes I know. *[Pause]* How was it?

WEBB: It was great.

VIOLET: I hear the parma's very good.

WEBB: Yes. But you can't eat the chips otherwise it's too filling. Do you like chicken parma?

VIOLET: I'm vegetarian.

WEBB: Oh. Sorry.

VIOLET: No. It's fine.

WEBB: Actually, they do have an eggplant parma if you like eggplant.

VIOLET: I don't really. Which is odd for a vegetarian.

WEBB: You know that in Italy, in Parma, they have never heard of a chicken parma. But they do have eggplant parma.

VIOLET: What about veal parma?

WEBB: I don't know. Probably not.

VIOLET: It probably wasn't the best time for Emmeline to pounce on you both with a new play.

WEBB: Oh. That's what it was. No. Probably not.

They laugh awkwardly. More silence. Finally, HELENA swoops in to break it.

HELENA: OK, let's have a look at this play.

WEBB: I think the horse has bolted on that one.

HELENA: What do you mean? Where's Emmy?

WEBB: She stormed off 'fuck sake-ing'.

HELENA: Whatever for?

WEBB: For art's sake, no doubt.

HELENA	*[To VIOLET]* We didn't meet properly back there. I'm Helena.
VIOLET:	*[A chancer]* Not Helena?
HELENA:	Well, aren't you just a delight! Come and sit down here immediately.
WEBB:	Helena, this is Violet and she has called your entire persona out in roughly thirty seconds. You have obviously met your match, so I advise you to go quietly with this one.
VIOLET:	I'm sorry that was a bit cocky. I don't really know what came over me.
HELENA:	Emmy I expect.
WEBB:	Lena!
VIOLET:	Well, it's true, in a sense. She did tell me about your stage name. I think it's really clever. But it was stupid of me to come out with it. I'm nervous, I think.
HELENA:	What have you got to be nervous about? Are you anxious about Emmy's play?
VIOLET:	Not really. I don't really understand it so it's difficult to be nervous about. No, I'm nervous about meeting you.
HELENA:	Oh really?
WEBB:	And suddenly all is forgiven.

VIOLET: I'm majoring in theatre studies at uni and I've been studying your career.

HELENA: What a coincidence! What subject?

VIOLET: Australian Theatre.

HELENA: Of course. That's fascinating. Contemporary practice?

VIOLET: No, history.

WEBB: Need to know basis, I suggest, Violet.

VIOLET: Of course, it is really more recent history.

HELENA: You are very sweet. But you are right. There's no escaping it. I suppose within the scope of Australian theatre I am now something of an historical character.

WEBB: Careful there, darling. This one's not been vetted.

VIOLET: Well, I don't think that is true.

HELENA: What? You mean you don't think I am an historic character?

VIOLET: Well I don't think you are old and washed-up, if that is what you are thinking.

WEBB: You are nervous. 'Old', 'washed-up' and calling out the stage name ruse are the three things we never mention in this house.

HELENA: Shut up Webby and listen to the woman.

VIOLET: I'm sorry. I really am on a spree today. But I think this whole business of retiring off women in the theatre the moment their boobs drop is really disgusting. Not to mention a waste of resources.

HELENA: I don't know what you mean.

VIOLET: You are not a 'historical character' you are an... Icon. No, that's not it either.

HELENA: You wouldn't say?

VIOLET: No, that's all just media speak and hype. You are an actor, pure and simple. You can do anything from Portia to Jimmy Porter.

HELENA: Well, perhaps not quite everything.

VIOLET: That's rubbish. When you did that Dickens thing you played about a hundred parts, men, women and children, all in one show without batting an eyelid. What on Earth makes you think you can't do just whatever you put your hand to?

HELENA: Well, it's not that I think that so much. It's more a matter of producers and directors and casting agents.

WEBB: Not to mention the call of Nature.

VIOLET: But what do you care about them? You don't need comfy theatres, blinged-up audiences and bean counters. Find a space, send out a few emails and get to it, woman. You did it in your Rear Four days.

HELENA: *[In a daze]* "Thou Nature art MY goddess."

VIOLET: Exactly.

WEBB: Now you really are sounding like Emmy.

VIOLET: Only when she is right.

HELENA: 'To me Thy services are bound.'

WEBB: That's your line, not Shakespeare's.

VIOLET: But the sentiment is spot on. Bugger Shakespeare.

HELENA: *[Off in a daze]* Yes. Bugger Shakespeare. Webby, I do think we need to mix things up a bit. Sydney's coming up. Let's do something different for a change. Cancel the STC and we can look for a bar somewhere. This is exactly the opportunity I have been thinking about.

WEBB: That's news to me.

VIOLET: Fantastic. This could be really exciting. I must arrange to come up to see you.

WEBB: That would be ideal. Wouldn't it, Lena? *[Pause]* Lena?

HELENA: *[Long gone]* Lovely.

There is a pause and a long silence.

VIOLET: What were we just saying about eggplant parma?

WEBB: I really don't remember.

After a beat, EMMELINE storms on and grabs the seated VIOLET by the arms and raises her off the couch.

EMMELINE: Violet! You were magnificent. *[Again with the aggressive kiss on the mouth]* We must go and have sex immediately.

EMMELINE grabs VIOLET by the hand and drags her off stage.

VIOLET: *[In transit]* Bye!

WEBB: Good bye, love.

HELENA is still on cloud nine and notices nothing.

End Act.

ACT TWO

HELENA's dressing room in a Sydney theatre. Some months have passed. HELENA is taking off her make-up after the show. This process goes on for some time and is a charming and insightful portrait of both the artist at work and the person on her own. Eventually WEBB enters with VIOLET. HELENA sees neither of them.

WEBB: Leni, someone is here.

HELENA: Please not tonight. I'm tired and I just want to go home to bed.

VIOLET: I'm sorry. I can come back tomorrow.

HELENA: *[Wheeling around]* Violet? Is that you?

VIOLET: It is. Hello.

HELENA: That's odd. Do you know I thought I saw you in the audience one night about three weeks ago.

VIOLET: You probably did. I have been in Sydney for about a month and I've popped in on the show now and again to see how it's been going.

WEBB: That's it. I knew I saw you.

HELENA: How many times have you seen it?

VIOLET: A couple of times.

HELENA: You should have come and said hello.

VIOLET: I tried at the opening, but it was far too busy. You wouldn't have noticed me. There were so many people back here.

HELENA: Well, come and sit down and tell me how brilliantly I have been doing. This whole thing was your idea, you know.

WEBB: And I thought this was going to be an early night.

VIOLET: No. I don't want to stop you getting some rest. I just wanted to say hi.

WEBB: Stay Violet. Rest is not what she needs now. What she needs now is jam.

VIOLET: Jam? Helena doesn't need jam.

WEBB: *[Kissing HELENA]* Good night dear. Don't stay up all night.

HELENA: Good night, Jam man.

WEBB: Good night, Violet. *[Moving to kiss her]* I know we are in the theatre, but are we really on kissing terms yet? I hope so.

VIOLET: We are.

WEBB: Good. *[At the door]* And by the way, Violet my love, 'Lesson One: Everyone Needs Jam.' *[He exists]*

HELENA: Webby, the philosopher. Your own?

WEBB: *[Off]* Noel Pierce Coward, 1899-1973.

There is a moderately long pause while HELENA gets on with her make-up routine. VIOLET looks about her with fascination.

VIOLET: It's really exciting to be here.

HELENA: What are you doing in Sydney for a month? Aren't you missing uni?

VIOLET: My parents live up here and I am taking some time off.

HELENA: So, you can take a whole semester off, can you?

VIOLET: I'm not sure. I just decided to do it at the last moment.

HELENA: Good for you. It's the perfect time in your life to throw caution to the wind.

VIOLET: That's what I think. My parents are a bit bemused by it all, but I can usually talk them round pretty easily.

HELENA: So, what have you been doing?

VIOLET: Stalking theatre companies really. I got sick of studying and I wanted to get some hands-on experience. I've pretty much done the Melbourne thing, so I thought I would try my luck in Sydney.

HELENA: Have you seen much here? There doesn't seem to be that much on at the moment, which is wonderful for me.

VIOLET: I have seen a bit, but I've really been trying to get my courage up to put myself in front of some key people.

HELENA: Have you had any success?

VIOLET: No. This is really my first interview.

HELENA: Heavens! Is that what this is?

VIOLET: It may not be for you, but it feels like it for me.

HELENA: Violet, how many times have you seen this show?

VIOLET: A few times. It's a bit embarrassing.

HELENA: How embarrassing?

VIOLET: Almost every night embarrassing!

HELENA: For Heaven's sake. You poor girl! You must be bored out of your brain.

VIOLET: Don't think that about me. It's not that many shows.

HELENA: It's been at least twenty-five.

VIOLET: Only if you count the previews.

HELENA: Well, I count the previews.

VIOLET: No one else does. Besides that is what you do when you are a student. You bash yourself over the head with a play as many times as you can, then try to say something intelligent about it.

HELENA: Is that what this play is like for you?

VIOLET: It doesn't feel like that. It's extraordinary. And you are such a star in it.

HELENA: You are very kind.

VIOLET: No, I'm not. I'm telling the truth. I know you think I am just some little idiot, throwing away everything to follow you up here and do nothing else but see your play every night. But I was really excited when we first met all those months ago. I was so much in awe of you before I met you. When I finally got the chance, I couldn't believe that you let me talk, and you seemed really interested in what I had to say. Then when you acted like you were going to take up my suggestion I was astounded. I couldn't wait around in Melbourne and read about the whole thing in the paper. There was no way I could talk about it there with Emmeline. I had to chuck everything for a while and come here and hurl myself at it.

HELENA: *[Laughing]* Oh my God, listen to yourself.

VIOLET: What do you mean? Don't laugh at me.

HELENA: I'm sorry but for the sake of your future self, that day when you are 45 and brushing your teeth and you finally realise what an idiot you were at 21, I suggest we stop this right now.

VIOLET: Stop what?

HELENA: Stop this *All About Eve* routine.

VIOLET: What is *All About Eve*?

HELENA: It's a film.

VIOLET: I've never heard of it.

HELENA: Yes, but you know the scenario. You are telling me that you have dropped out of uni to follow your heart, and my circus caravan, in the hope against hope that I am so stupid and vain that I will submit to your flattery and obvious brilliance, give you a job and prime you for a career of fame and fortune – probably over my dead body.

VIOLET: That's not what I am doing at all.

HELENA: No, it's not what you are doing, it's what you are telling me you are doing. What you are actually doing is extending the Easter holidays by a few weeks, doing all your coursework online, popping into the theatre once a week and sitting in the most obvious seat in the house – probably paid for by your poor, bemused parents – to make sure I notice you.

VIOLET: That's not it at all.

HELENA: Violet, I can see that you don't think that is what you are doing, but believe me, you are. Can you honestly tell me that since you walked in here tonight everything you have said is completely true?

VIOLET: Nearly everything.

HELENA: Well, that is a start at least. You have twenty odd years of self-examining teeth brushing sessions to calculate the honesty gap. I suggest you pack up your little schemes, take them back to your parents' house, get into your jimjams and begin a new life of self-examination with at least three minutes of looking into the mirror while you brush your teeth – but not too vigorously though, you don't want to experience any gum trauma.

VIOLET: Please don't be cruel. I am just trying to get on and I am really excited by all this. All I really want is to be like you.

HELENA: Oh yes. And how far do you think you need to go to get there? What other breaches in the honesty gap do you need to make to achieve that rather pathetic ambition? Do you want to be my make-up artist? My dresser? As you have obviously been messing about with my daughter, I'm not going to offer you the usual shortcut and start sleeping with you.

VIOLET: I'm not messing about with Emmeline. She just puts all that on, probably for your benefit. She's actually been at it for ages with that *Theatre Journal* boy. I know what it is that she likes to pretend, but her sex life has nothing to do with me. Nor much to do with him, I suspect.

HELENA: Oh, why didn't you say so? In that case we may as well get down to it right away. There's a couch over there, hop on and I'll join you.

VIOLET: I'm sorry. I have been a bit silly. But I don't know anything about this. What am I supposed to do? It's really hard to know where to begin.

HELENA: Well, you don't begin with me and you certainly don't begin like this. I have had quite enough of you girls and your mentor entitlement. I have seen it all before. I'm sick of the flattery and the envy and all the bony little arses being dangled in my face. If one more little wannabe ingénue walks in here with her boobs stuck out and her belly button sucked in I'm going to do something really vicious. I'm not a boy. It doesn't impress me.

VIOLET: *[Bursts into tears]* I'm sorry. I have been completely stupid.

HELENA: You have been stupid, but not in the way you think.

VIOLET: What do you mean?

HELENA: You have been silly to think this kind of approach gives you a chance with anything. If you had been here "almost every night" you would have known that most Tuesdays to Thursdays we are empty – and that is just the start. As for me, you have no idea about me, or what I do, or, more importantly, what I can do for you. Tell me honestly what you think about me.

VIOLET: Well, I know that you are successful. I know that you have had a long career, here and overseas, doing all sorts of interesting things.

HELENA: And that's what you want, is it?

VIOLET: Yes.

HELENA: But you know what it is really like don't you? Surely you have learned enough in your theatre studies subjects to know what that all really amounts to?

VIOLET: I know what you are going to say. You are going to give me all that stuff about an average of one show a year and terrible pay and huge breaks between shows and sucking up to producers and begging for work. I know about all that.

HELENA: But it's not 'stuff' if it's true.

VIOLET: I know it is true. But you haven't done too badly out of it. However much of a struggle you have had, you seem to have come out of it on top. That's what I want.

HELENA: On top! I don't have a cent to my name, I have never been able to maintain a relationship for more than about two weeks and I fully expect to be begging for work and sucking up to producers well into my seventies. *[Pause, VIOLET says nothing]* But that doesn't have any effect on you, does it? It doesn't matter how much I tell you that your ideas of my life are really only a fantasy. You just have this fixed idea of what I am, and that's what you want. I may as well not be here at all.

VIOLET: Well, perhaps I see your life for what it really is, rather than what you think it is.

HELENA: Oh my God. You really don't get to say that, you know. That really is incredibly arrogant, not to mention utterly moronic.

VIOLET: Well, it's better than being smug.

HELENA: Smug? How on Earth is *[indicates herself]* this smug?

VIOLET: You don't really get it, do you? You can walk down the street every day and on every corner someone recognises you and knows who you are. Then you get to go home and complain about it and whinge about not getting paid properly and having to beg for your next show. Can't you see how smug that is?

HELENA: But they don't know who I am and what I am really doing. On the very few occasions that I do get noticed, people say things to me that make that more than obvious.

VIOLET: But at least you get that.

HELENA: But it's horrendous. In fact, it's incredibly depressing. I did a few shows of some interest years ago. For stupid reasons some of those were picked up in the media on slow news days and I got my face splashed about a bit. My fifteen minutes of fame got stretched out into fifteen years of 'Oh I know her' and the bloody internet made some of that stupid stuff hang around for a few years more. Based on that nothing very much, you say I should be grateful? You don't really know what you are saying. It doesn't make me grateful, it makes me resentful. I don't live in the glow of celebrity. I live in the full knowledge of that thing you want, and what I suppose I always wanted, and how whatever that thing is, seems to be continually moving away from me. And you want me to teach you?

VIOLET: If not you who else?

HELENA: But that is what really scares me. This is the thing that really keeps me up at night. And it is not just you, it is Emmeline as well, and every one of the hot new things in the cast that pop on stage for the next few minutes. I don't have anything for you. For any of you. I can't give you anything. I am getting older and slower and I'm thoroughly burnt out. You imagine I have all these things you want, but I don't. I just don't.

VIOLET goes up to her and puts her arms about HELENA as she slouches on the table.

VIOLET: I'm sure that's not true. I know it's not true. It can't be.

End Act.

ACT THREE

As in Act One. Some weeks have passed. EMMELINE is sitting working madly at the laptop and WEBB is next to her browsing through the newspaper.

WEBB: Oh where is she?

EMMELINE: *[Not looking up]* How do I know? How do I ever know about Helena?

WEBB: We were supposed to be there half an hour ago.

EMMELINE: Do you honestly care whether you go or not?

WEBB: I have no desire to go. But she should – especially after what happened in Sydney.

EMMELINE: What did happen in Sydney?

WEBB: What do you mean?

EMMELINE: What do you mean?

WEBB: Well... the show.

EMMELINE: Was it really that bad?

WEBB: No one came. The reviews were terrible.

EMMELINE: One I read was all right. I was surprised.

WEBB: I don't think the *Green Left Weekly* really counts, do you?

EMMELINE: *[Smiling]* It does if you are a rainforest or an ecosystem.

WEBB: Maybe it does then. I am sure some critic or other once referred to your mother as a 'natural phenomenon'.

EMMELINE: Freak of nature perhaps. *[They go on reading and writing for a moment. Suddenly EMMELINE comes across something on a website]* Oh my god! What? It can't be!

WEBB: What is it?

EMMELINE: Oh my God! There's a Instagram post here with a picture of Violet... she looks like she's cut herself... and she's got a sign around her neck saying... What is it? "Leni made me do it."

WEBB: *[Jumping up]* Let me look at it.

EMMELINE: *[On the phone]* Pick up. Come on.

WEBB: Is that really her?

EMMELINE: *[Trying another number]* Yes. Marco? And what I want to know is why is that hanging around her neck. *[On phone]* Did you send me that? *[Listening]* Is it real? *[Listening]* I can't get her on the phone. *[Listening]* Well, is she alright? *[Listening]* Oh God. Call me if you hear from her. *[Listening]*. No. Not for months, you know that. *[Listening]*. Call me then. *[Hangs up]* It is her. She's in Sydney apparently. She tried to cut herself and then she posted it. It was all over the internet. They have just taken it down apparently.

WEBB: Did she really do it?

EMMELINE: I don't know. It looks pretty convincing. Marco thinks it's just a stunt but, you know her... *[Receives a text]* Hang on. She's OK. Pathetic attempt apparently.

WEBB: That's a relief.

EMMELINE: I didn't think she had it in her.

WEBB: What?

EMMELINE: She's hardly the drama queen is she?

WEBB: You think?

EMMELINE: I don't know, I suppose. Anyway, I haven't seen her for months. I don't know what she's been doing.

WEBB: You know we saw her in Sydney?

EMMELINE: What? You never said.

WEBB: I've hardly seen you. Didn't Leni tell you?

EMMELINE: No. Then again, it's not usually the sort of detail she retains.

WEBB: Well, it was hardly a detail. She was with us for weeks.

EMMELINE: What do you mean 'with' you?

WEBB: At the show.

EMMELINE: What was she doing at the show?

WEBB: I don't know, just hanging about and helping out.

EMMELINE: I had no idea.

WEBB: I am surprised your mother never mentioned it.

EMMELINE: Nothing surprises me about her. Anyway, it's Violet's story that perplexes me. What was she up to?

WEBB: When did you last see her?

EMMELINE: It was just before you left to do the show. I went into her room one morning and she was gone. She never said anything. She didn't even pack her stuff. We all called her but no one could find her. She just vanished. How long after that did she turn up in Sydney?

WEBB: It must have been pretty soon after because she sort of hung around for a few weeks before showing herself.

EMMELINE: What does that mean?

WEBB: Well, funnily enough, we thought we saw her once or twice in the house. Then one night she turned up and, apparently, she had been coming to the show off and on for a few weeks.

EMMELINE: That is totally weird. What on earth was she thinking?

WEBB: I thought it was pretty strange too. But then after a few days I kind of got used to her and didn't think anything of it. You know the kind of freaks that hang around backstage.

EMMELINE: What was she... kind of... obsessed with Helena or something?

WEBB: I don't think so. I mean she might have been a bit in awe of her at first, but it didn't seem to be anything really weird.

EMMELINE: Coming from you, who have been hanging around her for twenty years, that is not really saying much.

WEBB: Yeah, for a percentage, darling.

EMMELINE: That's what you tell yourself. Anyway, what happened?

WEBB: Nothing. She just hung about the show for a while, until we really did grind to a halt and then when we came home she stayed in Sydney with her parents.

EMMELINE: What? Her parents are not in Sydney. They are dead.

WEBB: What? She definitely said she was staying with her parents. Well, at least I think that is what she said.

We hear HELENA coming home.

EMMELINE: Sounds like she dudded you too, Webby. They died about five years ago – car crash. *[Calling]* Mum? Are you there?

HELENA: *[Off]* Yes. But I can't stop. Webby will be here in a minute and we are terribly late.

WEBB: *[Calling]* I am here and we are beyond late.

EMMELINE: *[Calling]* You better come and look at this. Mum?

HELENA: *[Off]* What?

WEBB: *[Calling]* Leni, come here this is important.

HELENA enters dressing, obviously annoyed.

HELENA: What on earth is it?

EMMELINE: Look.

HELENA: Darling, we're running really late. I don't have time to spend hours watching the You Tubes.

EMMELINE: It's not on YouTube, it's a post on Instagram.

HELENA comes around behind EMMELINE to see what it is.

HELENA: What am I looking at?

EMMELINE: Don't you recognise her?

HELENA: It's a shocking photo. *[Realises what it is]* Oh God. That's...

EMMELINE: It's Violet.

HELENA: Well, what is she doing? And who is 'Leni'?

EMMELINE: It's not you is it, Helena?

HELENA: Why would it be me? I hardly know the girl.

EMMELINE: Well, she's been with you all these months, hasn't she?

HELENA: What do you mean 'with' me?

WEBB: I told Emmie that Violet was helping us out in Sydney. Really, Leni, you should keep your daughter better informed.

HELENA: Well, what is the situation with this photo?

EMMELINE: It's all over the web, Mother.

WEBB: Yes, but she's OK. It sounds to me like it was a bit of a stupid joke. Didn't you think that Emmie?

EMMELINE: Possibly. In any case, she is all right.

HELENA: It sounds like a really sick joke. I just don't understand you kids and the way you put it all out there on the internet.

EMMELINE: Well I don't, and I don't recall Violet ever being really into that sort of thing.

HELENA: Well she did seem a bit unstable when we saw her in Sydney. All that business of hanging around the show for weeks before she decided to show her face. You can't say that was exactly normal behaviour.

EMMELINE: Yes, that did seem a little weird. And it was certainly very odd the way she just up and left the house like she did. But that doesn't exactly explain why she has your name stuck on a sign around her neck. Does it?

HELENA: My name? That's not my name.

EMMELINE: That's what he calls you. Don't you, Webby?

HELENA: Only very rarely and never when we have company.

EMMELINE: It's only a term of endearment, Mum, it's not a S and M codeword.

HELENA: I don't know what you are talking about.

WEBB: She is just teasing.

EMMELINE: No, I am not. I just want to know why my girlfriend has posted a photo of herself, cutting her wrists and with a sign around her neck with my mother's name on it?

HELENA: Your girlfriend! That's not what I heard. You are the weird one. From all reports you have been carrying on with the awkward theatre magazine boy. All Violet was to you was some sort of lesbag.

EMMELINE: And how do you come to know about that, Mum? That's a fairly personal piece of information about me for you to have bothered yourself about.

HELENA: Violet told me when we were in Sydney. And it is hardly a piece of intimate information.

EMMELINE: It is for me. It doesn't exactly make me comfortable to know that my mother is having those kinds of conversations with my closest friend. Especially as she never told me.

HELENA: Well, that doesn't mean any of this has anything to do with me.

WEBB: No one said anything like that, Leni.

HELENA: That's what she's saying. Aren't you Emmeline?

EMMELINE: Not exactly. So long as you are sure?

HELENA: Of course I am sure.

EMMELINE: So, you don't have any problem with this buzzing all around the net?

HELENA: Is it? I can't see why anyone would be interested.

EMMELINE: So long as she hasn't killed herself.

WEBB: *[Checking his phone]* Hang on, Emmie. We know she hasn't done anything of the sort.

EMMELINE: But that would be a story.

WEBB: But it's not the story. Stop sexing the whole thing up just to tease your mother. There is nothing to worry about, Leni. I am sure no one could make anything of it. It is really just a matter of a very disturbed young woman making a spectacle of herself. Leave it alone, Emmie. Anyway, I am going to leave you two in peace. We have well and truly missed that opening, Leni. I suggest we regroup tomorrow morning and assess the damage. *[HELENA has gone quiet, lost in thought]* Leni?

HELENA: Oh. Yep. Tomorrow.

WEBB: Thank you.

He turns and leaves. EMMELINE has noticed what has gone on. She waits a moment, then turns and follows him out

EMMELINE: *[Off]* Hang on a minute, Webby.

HELENA is still lost in thought. Soon enough her phone starts buzzing and buzzing and each time she looks at it and puts it down it buzzes again.

End Act.

ACT FOUR

Some time has passed. EMMELINE and HELENA are at breakfast, obviously in some holiday location and dressed in summer clothes.

EMMELINE: Mum, when are you going back to work?

HELENA: *[Head in the paper]* We only just got here.

EMMELINE: It's been nearly three weeks.

HELENA: Hardly an epic-length holiday.

EMMELINE: It is for you. Usually after about a week you start fantasising about letters from your public demanding your immediate return to the stage.

HELENA: Do I?

EMMELINE: You do. In fact, I can't think of any holiday we ever had lasting more than about ten days at most.

HELENA: Wearing you out, am I, with your endless sessions of reading on the beach and lunchtime nanna napping?

EMMELINE: Not exactly. I'm just not used to all this maternal quality time.

HELENA: You're always complaining we never do enough together.

EMMELINE: I'm not complaining. I'm just wondering how much of it there's going to be, so that I can psych myself up for the next bit.

HELENA: Well, it's not as if I have to rush back to work. I'm not exactly batting away the offers.

EMMELINE: Webby not doing his job then?

HELENA: No. That's not Webby's job.

EMMELINE: What exactly is Webby's role in your entourage?

HELENA: I don't know. Come to think of it, I can't really see what he does.

There is a short break in the conversation.

EMMELINE: Helena, what was Violet's job when she was in Sydney?

HELENA: *[Frustrated at being disturbed reading her paper]* Look Emmie, I don't want to go back to work. I need a break. There's no point rushing back to the city. I don't want to put my head up at the moment. If I do, I am bound to be asked to do things I don't want to do and stupid enough to agree to do them without thinking. I am tired. I just want some time here without the phone and people calling in, and without Webby 'looking out for my interests'. If you want to go back, go. But I am staying here.

EMMELINE: But why don't you want to stick you head up? That's different. You have never been like this before.

HELENA: Maybe I couldn't afford to before?

EMMELINE: Don't try that one on.

HELENA: I'm not trying anything on. I just need a holiday and I wish you would stop banging on about it. It is beginning to really annoy me.

EMMELINE: All right, I'll stop.

HELENA: At last.

They both resume the paper business. After a time EMMELINE's phone buzzes on the table and HELENA jumps a mile in the air.

EMMELINE: What's the matter? It's only my phone.

HELENA: I got the shock of my life. That's exactly why I don't want to go back to work. If I hear that again, I'll go nuts.

EMMELINE: I'll turn it off.

HELENA: Please do. *[They go on reading. Soon HELENA loses concentration and looks out over the ocean]* I was thinking about Violet the other day. You just mentioned her.

EMMELINE: I did.

HELENA: Did you ever do that play you were working on?

EMMELINE: No.

HELENA: That's a pity. Was it any good?

EMMELINE: It had its moments.

HELENA: *[Smiling]* Not quite up to your early work.

EMMELINE: Not quite.

HELENA: What was it about?

EMMELINE: Asylum seekers.

HELENA: Asylum seekers?

EMMELINE: Yes.

HELENA: Did Violet have anything to do with the writing?

EMMELINE: Nothing. In fact she had very little to do with it at all. I had this stupid idea about it all being a kind of non-performance. So, she pretty much just stood there and spoke the lines.

HELENA: A non-performance?

EMMELINE: That's right. Stupid really.

HELENA: So, what you are saying is that it was really all about me?

EMMELINE: Surprisingly not.

HELENA: Because you know I do have a lot to do with the asylum seeker issues.

EMMELINE: Yeah right. Even I couldn't miss your benefit performance. Although what exactly 'Blow Gabriel Blow' has to do with refugees still manages to escape me.

HELENA: We all do our bit in our own way, my love.

EMMELINE: I suppose that is true.

HELENA: Was she any good at it? Violet?

EMMELINE: We hardly had a chance to find out. She threw me over for you and Sydney before we even got into the theatre. I had to do it.

HELENA: What do you mean threw you over for me?

EMMELINE: That's what it was, wasn't it Mum?

HELENA: No. I don't think so.

EMMELINE: Well, what was it?

HELENA: I don't really know. I don't know what she was thinking. I assume she was looking for an opportunity, of some sort or other, and tried on the Eve Harrington routine with me.

EMMELINE: Did you fall for it?

HELENA: Of course. Margo always falls for Eve Harrington. Every single night.

EMMELINE: But why, particularly when you obviously know it's coming? Is your ego really that fragile?

HELENA: You seem to think it is. All that stuff about 'Dame Helena'.

EMMELINE: If you are allowed to cling to type, I should be able to do it occasionally. But I really don't think your ego is that fragile. In fact, I think you are pretty tough, which is why I don't see how you could fall for Violet's routine.

HELENA: I am pretty tough, but I am surprised you have noticed it. I always feel at my most fragile when I am with you. It is all the rest of the time that I feel I have to put a face on it.

EMMELINE: So, what happened with Violet?

HELENA: I suppose for once I had to see what would happen if I did something really reckless.

EMMELINE: Reckless and heartless.

HELENA: Why heartless?

EMMELINE: You never really considered how I would feel about it. Or was that part of the reckless bit?

HELENA: You and Violet? I thought that was all fooling? You are not really telling me it was love?

EMMELINE: Well, it wasn't exactly *Flames of Passion* but it had its moments.

HELENA: Did it? *[Pause]* Did it? I'm sorry. I didn't think that was possible. Actually, I may have been heartless, but I am not really sure about the reckless bit. Perhaps it was more like not stopping myself from doing something unthinkable. That is different for me. I know you think I just faff about on stage and make it up as I go along, but I really don't. You do because you have the talent, but I have to work. I doubt I really do anything on stage, or anywhere else, without planning it and thinking at least two or three plot points ahead of myself. When it came to Violet I am not sure whether it was planned or whether, for the first time in my life, I just did nothing to resist. Of course, I'd like to think it was planned – I think everyone needs to do something really reprehensible at least once in life, especially an actor – but I just don't know.

EMMELINE: Did you fall in love with her?

HELENA: No.

EMMELINE: Really?

HELENA: No. I think you need to feel at least something coming back to you, on a sustained basis, for that to happen.

EMMELINE: So, was it just about the sex?

HELENA: Who said anything about sex?

EMMELINE: You don't seem to be implying that it wasn't about sex.

HELENA: You don't think I am capable of the same relationship with Violet that you had?

EMMELINE: So, you do think that is possible?

HELENA: Of course I do. But it is rarely practical. It is usually an expected part of the give and take of relationship politics.

EMMELINE: So, it was about the sex.

HELENA: Let's just say it had its moments.

EMMELINE: Fair enough. But if it wasn't about the reckless, or the heartless, or the sex, what could it have been about?

HELENA: Something tells me you have a theory.

EMMELINE: I do, as a matter of fact, but I doubt you will like it.

HELENA: Why not?

EMMELINE: In a way it is about the end of your career.

HELENA: Isn't that what all your theories are about? I have read your journal.

EMMELINE: This isn't about theory. This is about what you actually do. Or don't do anymore.

HELENA: How comforting.

EMMELINE: Remember that show we did when you dragged me out of Year Ten to go on the road with you?

HELENA: That was our only show – how could I forget?

EMMELINE: That was an astounding experience for me.

HELENA: I know. For you it was the beginning of the end.

EMMELINE: Yes, but it really taught me a lot. I had no confidence, no timing, I had no real idea what I was doing and it was all just passing along in a blur. But when I was in the scenes with you, I felt I was in total control and all my choices seemed to be the right ones. You don't realise how much you give an actor on stage. I have heard lots of actors say this. When I was acting with you, you had this ability to look me in the eye, right in the middle of a scene, and that look seemed to tell me what to do. Or rather it seemed to give me the confidence to follow my instincts, which is even better. Absolutely invaluable to work with.

HELENA: So, what has that to do with Violet?

EMMELINE: With Violet you probably realised that it has gone. Or at least that it is going. It is the end of your career because you can't do it anymore. The young actor on stage looks to you and all you have for her is a cold, dark incomprehensible stare. No one is getting anywhere with that. That is why you had to take the whole thing off in another, less professional, direction. "When you were graveled for lack of matter, you took occasion to kiss!"

HELENA: "Very good orators, when they are out, they will spit..."

EMMELINE: Exactly. So, I am right?

HELENA: Oh, I don't know. Maybe. Though I don't really think I am all that washed-up. At least I think I am still good for a cue or two, and the odd one-liner.

EMMELINE: Not much good for the likes of Violet I suspect.

HELENA: *[With regret]* No, I suppose not. *[Pause]* Nor you, I imagine. "I can't give you anything but love, baby!"

EMMELINE: That's all I ever wanted. But that was never really your thing.

HELENA: I know. I tried.

EMMELINE: Yes, I know. It has always been good enough for me.

HELENA: Has it? That is something. I didn't know.

End Act.

Act Five

The same seaside town, although some years have passed. EMMELINE is seated on a lounge chair overlooking the ocean. WEBB is seated on the edge of another chair, clearly not in holiday mode, with papers and pens about him.

WEBB: Here, sign this.

EMMELINE: What is it?

WEBB: That's just cleaning up the tax business.

EMMELINE: So that's it?

WEBB: Pretty much.

EMMELINE: For such an impractical woman she certainly had a lot going on business wise.

WEBB: That was pretty much my fault.

EMMELINE: She was lucky you did your job and so am I now. *[She signs the paper with a sense of occasion]* So that's it?

WEBB: And it only took us a year.

EMMELINE: She died a year ago? I suppose she did. Doesn't seem so long as that. I've hardly had time to miss her.

WEBB: That will come, no doubt.

EMMELINE: What about you Webby? Do you miss her?

WEBB: I have hardly had the time. I guess it will come. We were together such a long time. With a woman like your mother there's always so much to digest between meetings. Perhaps I am still working on that from a year ago.

EMMELINE: Gastric juices frothing away, eh?

WEBB: What about you?

EMMELINE: Missing Helena? Not really. Not any more than I ever did when she was alive. I am sad that she has gone when I think about it. But the rest of the time it hardly feels like she has gone at all. It's like in the old days, when you never really knew where or when she was going to pop up. Apart from that, I didn't really have the same expectations of her that you probably had. We never really got to know each other, not like you two did.

WEBB: Did we? I wonder?

EMMELINE: Well, you certainly had more time with her than I did. To be honest I can only really remember one or two conversations we ever had about anything in particular, anything real.

WEBB: And what were they like?

EMMELINE: Surprising.

WEBB: Well, I don't know anything about parenthood, but I would have thought that to achieve 'surprising' is pretty much 'job done'.

EMMELINE: I suppose so.

Enter MADELEINE in something of a hurry.

MADELEINE: Emmy, quick give me the beach ball. There are a couple of little kids here and I want to trap them into playing a game before their mum decides to cart them off.

EMMELINE: Maddie, slow down and say hello to this fellow.

MADELEINE: Hello there, chap.

WEBB: Hello to you.

MADELEINE: *[To EMMELINE]* He seems a business-like type of fellow. Who is he?

EMMELINE: He is a business-like type of fellow and without him none of us would probably be here.

MADELEINE: Why, is he your dad? *[To WEBBY]* You're not are you?

WEBB: Not in the slightest.

EMMELINE: Don't take any notice of her Webby.

MADELEINE: Yes, I wouldn't take too much notice of me. My Year Five teacher once told me that I had an unnatural obsession with "obscure theatrical parentage situations" – it's because almost half of my female relatives seem to have no idea who their actual fathers are. It's not my fault.

WEBB: Well, as long as you know who your father is.

MADELEINE: *[Suspiciously]* I do.

EMMELINE: Well, at least there's no mystery about who her grandmother is.

WEBB: Yes, I can see that. And brother Alan is the lucky father?

MADELEINE: He is, as a matter of fact. Although I wouldn't tell too many people that, if I were you.

WEBB: Why not?

MADELEINE: I need something of a family scandal to pad out my background. You know, to give me a leg up in the business. No point them thinking I come from some dull old unbroken family in the suburbs. I'll never get anywhere.

EMMELINE: Maddie, enough. Here, take the ball and try to behave like a normal child for five minutes at least.

MADELEINE: All right, I'm off.

EMMELINE: Hang on. Which one is the mother?

MADELEINE: That tall good-looking one with the yellow thing around her bum.

EMMELINE: Well, go and make sure it is OK with her first. Those kids are much younger than you.

MADELEINE: *[To WEBB]* Cheerio chap. I'm off. Remember to keep your trap shut about the Alan situation. It's a need to know basis.

She leaves with the ball.

WEBB: Most amusing. Can't think why I never had one.

EMMELINE: You are telling me.

WEBB: I can see why you don't miss Helena while you have that one hanging about.

EMMELINE: She's staying with me for the week.

WEBB: By the way, have you had a good look at the tall, good-looking one with the yellow thing around her bum?

EMMELINE: No.

WEBB: Well do. She's just walking up the beach now.

EMMELINE: Is that...?

WEBB: I'm pretty sure it is.

He collects up his things.

EMMELINE: You are not going. This is bound to be fascinating.

WEBB: I am as a matter of fact. After Madeleine's intervention I think I have had all the fascination I can take today.

He exits. VIOLET enters.

EMMELINE: I thought that was you.

VIOLET: Me too. My God, Emmeline, I haven't seen you since *[Pauses to think]* since ages.

EMMELINE: You are right. It has been years.

VIOLET: Not since we lived in that house in Collingwood.

EMMELINE: Yes. In fact, I think I still have some of your stuff.

VIOLET: Oh really? What? Oh, was that one of those places I skipped out on?

EMMELINE: Not exactly. I mean, I don't think you left any unpaid rent or bills or anything like that.

VIOLET: Well, that's something at least. I did walk out and leave one or two bad situations behind me I think.

EMMELINE: Well, it was such a long time ago. I am sure anything like that is long forgotten.

VIOLET: Do you think? I hope so.

EMMELINE: Are they your kids?

VIOLET: Two of them are. I don't know who that lovely redhead is?

EMMELINE: She belongs to me.

VIOLET: That's your daughter?

EMMELINE: No, my niece. My brother's daughter.

VIOLET: I don't think I ever met your brother. I'm sorry.

EMMELINE: Don't apologise. I never met anyone of yours either.

VIOLET: Of course, I did all that research on your mum when I was at uni.

EMMELINE: Yes. You met her too. You knew her in Sydney.

VIOLET: That's right. Do you have any?

EMMELINE: Any children?

VIOLET: Yes.

EMMELINE: No.

VIOLET: Too busy doing plays probably?

EMMELINE: Not really. I am busy working, but that's not the reason I don't have children.

VIOLET: Sorry. Have I said something awkward?

EMMELINE: No. There's nothing awkward about it. I just never met someone I wanted to stay with long enough to have a child. But tell me about yours, you will enjoy the conversation much more.

VIOLET: You are funny. The older one is Grace and the boy is Pablo. The sleeping giant on the beach there is Ully. We've been married about three years.

EMMELINE: They are lovely. Are you working?

VIOLET: Only two days a week at the moment. I'm teaching drama at a primary school and it works out quite well because they had their funding cut. What about you?

EMMELINE: Still at the old stand. I am trying to keep the remains of the old family company going. Although Webby is still around to do all the business stuff. You remember him, don't you?

VIOLET: Freddy?

EMMELINE: No Webby. Cliff Webb. He was with my mother all those years. In fact, he was just here a minute ago.

VIOLET: No. I don't I am afraid. Strangely enough I was thinking about your mother the other day. How is she?

EMMELINE: Actually, she died about a year ago.

VIOLET: Oh God. I'm sorry.

EMMELINE: No. It is fine. You didn't know.

VIOLET: I didn't. I must have missed it in the papers – I never have time anymore.

EMMELINE: There wasn't much in the papers. She had been fairly quiet for the last few years.

VIOLET: Had she been ill? She was so young.

EMMELINE: Well, she had cancer, but it wasn't diagnosed until just before she died. No, I mean she had been quiet professionally.

VIOLET: That is really sad news. I am so sorry. She was a wonderful woman.

EMMELINE: She certainly thought so.

VIOLET: You are terrible. She was amazing. You were always so full on about your mother.

EMMELINE: She was amazing. I know I was pretty tough on her, but we had time to work most of it out before the end. I doubt I could have stood much more of her, but at least I felt I understood her.

VIOLET: She was such a significant figure. I know I hardly knew her, but she had such an inspiring career. I really tried to model myself on her, when I was at uni and in my five minutes of a career after that. Of course, I never told you that, you were so mad at her all the time. You don't mind me saying that?

EMMELINE: No. That was about right.

VIOLET: But she was really important as far as women in Australian theatre go. But you say that things went quiet for here in her last years?

EMMELINE: Sort of. Although I think it was more a case of her going quiet.

VIOLET: Not after that show in Sydney?

EMMELINE: Why do you say that?

VIOLET: No reason in particular. It had terrible reviews, although it was a really fantastic show and she was excellent in it. I suppose that kind of reception might have depressed anyone.

EMMELINE: No. There was nothing unusual about Helena getting dud reviews. She had plenty of those in her time. Although I suspect she did become depressed, for want of a better word.

VIOLET: What about? If not about work?

EMMELINE: Certainly she was pretty glum about the industry. Not much room for even the grands dames of the theatre. But I think it was something beyond that.

VIOLET: I assume she never married? Was she lonely?

EMMELINE: Never. She never complained about that. Actually, she never really complained about anything other than bad theatre. She just pulled out of things a fair bit and withdrew somewhat. She was never really redundant, in the strict sense of the word. I just think she felt it.

VIOLET: She could have reinvented herself in a minute.

EMMELINE: I suppose. But I think when you have spent fifty odd years inventing and reinventing yourself it is likely that you are going to want to settle on one of your personas.

VIOLET: I am really sorry to hear it. Sounds like an unhappy last few years.

EMMELINE: It was. But it could have been the cancer. Who knows?

Pause.

VIOLET: I have just had this terrible thought.

EMMELINE: What is it?

VIOLET: I had forgotten how terribly I behaved.

EMMELINE: What do you mean?

VIOLET: I forgot I did this completely stupid thing. Did you know?

EMMELINE: No. What was it?

VIOLET: I feel terrible.

EMMELINE: What was it?

VIOLET: Oh, I went through this incredibly self-destructive phase, about five or six years ago. I was really depressed and terribly worried about my future. I remember I had an audition in Sydney and the whole process tore me to shreds. It was a total failure. I didn't get the job, of course, and so I started lashing out at anyone who was near me. One night I got really drunk and posted a stupid photo of myself pretending to cut my wrists. Didn't you hear about it?

EMMELINE: No. I didn't.

VIOLET: Really? You don't remember it? Everyone else saw it?

EMMELINE: I've never really been into social networking.

VIOLET: Oh, it was so embarrassing. I made such a fool of myself.

EMMELINE: Sounds just like a stupid joke. I'm sure it didn't harm anyone.

VIOLET: You are probably right. Except that I am pretty sure I posted some text with it that was really bitchy about your mum.

EMMELINE: Really? What was it?

VIOLET: I can't remember it exactly.

EMMELINE: Why did you do that?

VIOLET: I don't know. I must have been crazy. It was after I was helping out on the show in Sydney and she had been really nice to me. It was an incredibly nasty thing to do. You don't think she saw it, do you?

EMMELINE: I am one hundred percent sure she didn't.

VIOLET: Really. But how do you know?

EMMELINE: She never really dealt with social networking. I doubt she would have even known how to find it. I fact once I asked her about Instagram and she thought it was some express service for scoring coke.

VIOLET: I hope not. I can't believe now that I was ever capable of doing something like that.

EMMELINE: I wouldn't worry. There's so much on the web no one can really find anything. Let alone Helena. No, I am sure she had no idea. She was so busy with everything, and then with the cancer, I'm sure she wouldn't have given it a moment's thought. Even if she had seen it.

CURTAIN.

www.ingramcontent.com/pod-product-compliance
Lightning Source LLC
Chambersburg PA
CBHW071318080526
44587CB00018B/3273